Catholic Family Prayers

Catholic Family Prayers

PARACLETE PRESS
BREWSTER, MASSACHUSETTS

2017 First Printing
Catholic Family Prayers
Copyright © 2017 by Paraclete Press, Inc.
ISBN 978-1-61261-972-9

Pope Francis's "Prayer to the Holy Family" excerpted from *Amoris Lætitia* and Pope St. John Paul II's "A Prayer for Every Family on Earth" copyright © Libreria Editrice Vaticana.
The Paraclete Press name and logo (dove on cross) are trademarks of Paraclete Press, Inc.

Library of Congress Cataloging-in-Publication Data
Names: Paraclete Press.
Title: Catholic family prayers.
Description: Brewster, Massachusetts : Paraclete Press Inc., 2017.
Identifiers: LCCN 2017031409 | ISBN 9781612619729 (trade paper)
Subjects: LCSH: Catholic Church—Prayers and devotions. |
Families—Prayers
   and devotions. | Prayers.
Classification: LCC BX2130 .C374 2017 | DDC 242/.802—dc23
LC record available at https://lccn.loc.gov/2017031409

Published by Paraclete Press
Brewster, Massachusetts
www.paracletepress.com

Printed in the United States of America

CONTENTS

Prayers by Saints

Prayers Through Saints

Special Prayers

Stations of the Cross

The Peace Prayer

INTRODUCTION

Catholic family life is infused with prayer. From table graces to the rosary, devotions, and creeds, Catholics grow up with prayer as a part of their religious life, and their daily routine. But too often, the noises and pressures of the world drown out the still, small voice of our heavenly Father.

Catholic Family Prayers is a collection of essential prayers for the Catholic family, organized in sections for easy reference. You and your family can use it to take advantage of opportunities to draw closer to the Lord and to each other in prayer. Remind yourself of prayers for specific occasions and keep those traditions alive, and discover new prayers for your family to learn and treasure.

Common Prayers

Our Father (The Lord's Prayer)

Our Father, who art in heaven,
hallowed be thy name.
Thy kingdom come.
Thy will be done, on earth as it is
in heaven.
Give us this day our daily bread.
And forgive us our trespasses,
as we forgive those who trespass
against us.
And lead us not into temptation,
but deliver us from evil. Amen.

Glory Be (Doxology)

Glory be to the Father,
and to the Son,
and to the Holy Spirit.
As it was in the beginning,
is now, and ever shall be,
world without end. Amen.

A slightly different version comes from the Liturgy of the Hours:

Glory to the Father, and to the Son,
and to the Holy Spirit.
As it was in the beginning, is now,
and will be forever. Amen.

Sign of the Cross

In the name of the Father
and of the Son
and of the Holy Spirit. Amen.

The Act of Contrition

My God,
I am sorry for my sins with all my heart.
In choosing to do wrong
and failing to do good,
I have sinned against you
whom I should love above all things.
I firmly intend, with your help,
to do penance,
to sin no more,
and to avoid whatever leads me to sin.
Our Savior Jesus Christ
suffered and died for us.
In his name, my God, have mercy.

The Nicene Creed

I believe in one God, the Father almighty, maker of heaven and
earth, of all things visible and invisible.

I believe in one Lord Jesus Christ, the Only Begotten Son of
God, born of the Father before all ages. God from God, Light
from Light, true God from true God, begotten, not made,
consubstantial with the Father; through him all things were
made. For us men and for our salvation he came down from
heaven, and by the Holy Spirit was incarnate of the Virgin
Mary, and became man.

For our sake he was crucified under Pontius Pilate, he suffered
death and was buried, and rose again on the third day in
accordance with the Scriptures. He ascended into heaven and
is seated at the right hand of the Father. He will come again
in glory to judge the living and the dead and his kingdom will
have no end.

I believe in the Holy Spirit, the Lord, the giver of life, who
proceeds from the Father and the Son, who with the Father
and the Son is adored and glorified, who has spoken through
the prophets.

I believe in one, holy, catholic and apostolic Church. I confess
one Baptism for the forgiveness of sins and I look forward to
the resurrection of the dead and the life of the world to come.
Amen.

The Apostles' Creed

I believe in God, the Father almighty, Creator of heaven and
earth, and in Jesus Christ, his only Son, our Lord: who was
conceived by the Holy Spirit, born of the Virgin Mary,
suffered under Pontius Pilate, was crucified, died and was
buried; he descended into hell; the third day he rose again
from the dead; he ascended into heaven, and is seated at the
right hand of God the Father almighty; from thence he shall
come to judge the living and the dead.

I believe in the Holy Spirit, the holy catholic Church, the
communion of saints, the forgiveness of sins, the resurrection
of the body, and life everlasting. Amen.

Table
Graces

Before Meals

Bless us, O Lord, and these thy gifts,
which we are about to receive from thy bounty.
Through Christ our Lord.
Amen.

Blessed are you, almighty Father,
who gives us our daily bread.
Blessed is your only begotten Son,
who continually feeds us with the Word of Life.
Blessed is the Holy Spirit,
who brings us together at this table of love.
Blessed be God now and forever.
Amen.

After Meals

We give thee thanks for all thy benefits, Almighty God,
who lives and reigns forever, world without end.
Amen.
And may the souls of the faithful departed,
through the mercy of God, rest in peace.
Amen.

Loving Father, we praise you for all the gifts you give us:
for life and health;
for faith and love;
and for this meal we have shared together.
Father, we thank you through Christ our Lord.
Amen.

God, our Father,
we thank you for the food your bounty has given us,
your gathered family.
Grant that we also may freely give to others
what you have so generously given to us,
and that we may all share in the banquet of heaven.
We ask this through Christ our Lord.
Amen.

Prayers for Morning

Morning Offering

O Jesus, through the Immaculate Heart of Mary,
I offer you my prayers, works, joys, and sufferings of this day
for all the intentions of your Sacred Heart,
in union with the Holy Sacrifice of the Mass throughout the
world,
for the salvation of souls, the reparation for sins, the reunion
of all Christians,
and in particular for the intentions of the Holy Father.
Amen.

Guardian Angel Prayer

Angel of God,
my guardian dear,
To whom God's love
commits me here,
Ever this day,
be at my side,

To light and guard,
Rule and guide.
Amen.

Before Work

May God bless the work
I will do this day,
that all my actions
may bring Christ to the world.

God be in my head and in my understanding;
God be in my eyes and in my looking;
God be in my mouth and in my speaking;
God be in my heart and in my thinking;
God be at my end, and at my departing.

For a Child Leaving for School

May God bless your day at school,
that you may grow
in knowledge of the world,
and in love for all God's children.

Prayers
for Evening

Prayer for a Child Before Bed

As you make the sign of the cross on the child's forehead or heart:

May God bless you.
May God keep you safe.
God be with you.
God be in your heart.
May God bless and protect you.

Night Prayer of St. Augustine

Watch, Lord, with those who wake or weep tonight. Give the angels and saints charge over those who sleep. O Lord Jesus Christ, tend your sick ones, rest your weary ones, bless your dying ones, soothe the suffering ones, pity all the afflicted ones, shield the joyful ones, and all for your love's sake. Amen.

Evening Prayer of St. Alphonsus Liguori

Jesus Christ, my God, I adore you and I thank you for the many graces you have bestowed on me this day. I offer you my sleep and all the moments of this night, and I pray you to preserve me from sin. Therefore, I place myself in your most sacred side, and under the mantle of our blessed Lady, my Mother. May the holy angels assist me and keep me in peace, and may your blessing be upon me.

Marian Prayers

Hail Mary

Hail Mary, full of grace,
the Lord is with thee.
Blessed art thou among women,
and blessed is the fruit of thy
womb, Jesus.
Holy Mary, Mother of God,
pray for us sinners,
now and at the hour of our death.
Amen.

The Magnificat

My soul proclaims the greatness of the Lord,
my spirit rejoices in God my Savior;
for he has looked with favor on his lowly servant.

From this day all generations will call me blessed:
the Almighty has done great things for me,
and holy is his Name.

He has mercy on those who fear him
in every generation.

He has shown the strength of his arm,
he has scattered the proud in their conceit.

He has cast down the mighty from their thrones,
and has lifted up the lowly.

He has filled the hungry with good things,
and the rich he has sent away empty.

He has come to the help of his servant Israel
for he has remembered his promise of mercy,
the promise he made to our fathers,
to Abraham and his children forever.

Memorare
(Traditional)

Remember, O most gracious Virgin Mary, that never was it
known that anyone who fled to thy protection, implored thy
help, or sought thine intercession was left unaided.

Inspired by this confidence, I fly unto thee, O Virgin of virgins,
my mother; to thee do I come, before thee I stand, sinful and
sorrowful. O Mother of the Word Incarnate, despise not my
petitions, but in thy mercy hear and answer me.
Amen.

Memorare
(Modern)

Remember, most loving Virgin Mary,
never was it heard
that anyone who turned to you for help
was left unaided.

Inspired by this confidence,
though burdened by my sins,
I run to your protection
for you are my mother.

Mother of the Word of God,
do not despise my words of pleading
but be merciful and hear my prayer.
Amen.

Angelus

This Marian prayer incorporates the "Hail Mary" and traditionally is recited at 6 AM, noon, and 6 PM—a practice maintained in many monastic communities. It is most common today for Catholics to recite the Angelus at 6 PM, as part of Vespers or by itself. It can be said alone, or if said in a group, the lines marked ℣ are read by the leader, those marked with ℟ by everyone else, and those unmarked by everyone.

℣. The Angel of the Lord declared unto Mary,
℟. And she conceived of the Holy Spirit.

Hail Mary, full of grace, the Lord is with thee. Blessed art thou among women, and blessed is the Fruit of thy womb, Jesus. Holy Mary, Mother of God, pray for us sinners, now and at the hour of our death.

℣. Behold the handmaid of the Lord.
℟. Be it done unto me according to thy word.

Hail Mary, full of grace, the Lord is with thee. Blessed art thou among women, and blessed is the Fruit of thy womb, Jesus. Holy Mary, Mother of God, pray for us sinners, now and at the hour of our death.

℣. And the Word was made flesh.
℟. And dwelt among us.

Hail Mary, full of grace, the Lord is with thee. Blessed art thou among women, and blessed is the Fruit of thy womb, Jesus. Holy Mary, Mother of God, pray for us sinners, now and at the hour of our death.

℣. Pray for us, O Holy Mother of God.
℟. That we might be made worthy of the promises of Christ.

℣. Let us pray.

Pour forth, we beseech thee, O Lord, thy grace into our hearts; that we, to whom the Incarnation of Christ, thy Son, was made known by the message of an angel, may by his Passion and Cross be brought to the glory of his Resurrection. Through the same Christ our Lord.

℟. Amen.

Marian
Antiphons

There are four Marian antiphons which traditionally are used at the end of final prayers of the day (Vespers or Compline). They vary seasonally, though now it is common to use them at any time of year.

They are:

Alma Redemptoris Mater
Advent through Saturday before Presentation of the Lord

Ave Regina Cælorum
Presentation of the Lord through Wednesday of Holy Week

Regina Cæli
Easter Season
Holy Saturday to Pentecost

Salve Regina
Trinity Sunday through Saturday before Advent

Alma Redemptoris Mater
(Loving Mother of Our Savior)

The Alma Redemptoris Mater *is one of the four seasonal antiphons of the Blessed Virgin Mary, traditionally sung during Advent and Christmas, at the end of final prayers of the day. The opening verses are attributed to Hermannus Contractus in the eleventh century.* Alma Redemptoris Mater *holds the distinction of being mentioned in Geoffrey Chaucer's Canterbury Tales. The popular English translation included here and in the following antiphons is by Fr. Edward Caswall.*

Mother of Christ! Hear thou thy people's cry,
Star of the deep, and portal of the sky!
Mother of him who thee from nothing made,
Sinking we strive and call to thee for aid;
Oh, by that joy which Gabriel brought to thee,
Thou Virgin first and last, let us thy mercy see.

(In Latin)
Alma Redemptoris Mater, quæ pervia cæli
Porta manes, et stella maris, sucurre cadenti,
Surgere qui curat populo: tu quæ genuisti,
Natura mirante, tuum sanctum Genitorem,
Virgo prius ac posterius, Gabrielis ab ore
Sumens illud Ave, peccatorum miserere.

The versicle, response, and prayer that follow come in two forms,
one for Advent and one for the Christmas season.

ADVENT

Versicle: The angel of the Lord declared unto Mary.
Response: And she conceived by the Holy Ghost.

Let us pray.
Pour forth we beseech thee, O Lord, thy grace into our hearts;
that as we have known the incarnation of Christ thy Son by
the message of an angel, so by his Passion and Cross we may
be brought to the glory of his resurrection; through the same
Christ, our Lord.
Amen.

(In Latin)
℣. Angelus Domini nuntiavit Mariæ.
℟. Et concepit de Spiritu Sancto.

Oremus.
Gratiam tuam, quæsumus, Domine, mentibus nostris infunde; ut, qui, angelo
nuntiante, Christi Filii tui incarnationem cognovimus, per passionem ejus
et crucem, ad resurrectionis gloriam perducamur. Per eumdem Christum
Dominum nostrum.
Amen.

CHRISTMAS SEASON

Versicle: After childbirth thou didst remain a pure virgin.
Response: O Mother of God, intercede for us.

Let us pray.
O God, who, by the fruitful virginity of Blessed Mary, hast
given unto mankind the rewards of eternal salvation: grant,
we beseech thee, that we may feel that she intercedes for us,
through whom we have been made worthy to receive the
Author of life, our Lord Jesus Christ, thy Son.
Amen.

(In Latin)
℣. *Post partum, Virgo, inviolata permansisti.*
℟. *Dei Genitrix, intercede pro nobis.*

Oremus.
Deus, qui salutis aeternæ, beatæ Mariæ virginitate fecunda, humano generi
præmia præstitisti: tribue, quæsumus, ut ipsam pro nobis intercedere sentiamus,
per quam meruimus auctorem vitæ suscipere, Dominum nostrum Iesum
Christum, Filium tuum.
Amen.

Ave Regina Cælorum

(Welcome, O Queen of Heaven)

The Ave Regina Cælorum is one of the four seasonal antiphons of the Blessed Virgin Mary, traditionally sung from the Feast of the Presentation until Wednesday of Holy Week, at the end of the final prayers of the day.

Hail, O Queen of Heaven enthroned.
Hail by angels mistress owned!
Root of Jesse, gate of morn,
From whom the world's true light was born.

Glorious Virgin, joy to thee!
Loveliest whom in heaven they see.
Fairest thou, where all are fair!
Plead with Christ our sins to spare.

℣. Vouchsafe that I may praise thee, O sacred Virgin.
℟. Give me strength against thine enemies.

Let us pray.
Grant, O merciful God, defense to our weakness; that we who now celebrate the memory of the holy Mother of God may, by the aid of her intercession, rise again from our sins. Through the same Christ our Lord.
Amen.

(In Latin)
Ave, Regina cælorum,
Ave, Domina Angelorum:
Salve, radix, salve, porta
Ex qua mundo lux est orta:
Gaude, Virgo gloriosa,
Super omnes speciosa,
Vale, o valde decora,
Et pro nobis Christum exora.

℣. *Dignare me laudare te, Virgo sacrata.*
℟. *Da mihi virtutem contra hostes tuos.*

Oremus.
Concede, misericors Deus, fragilitati nostræ præsidium: ut, qui sanctæ Dei
Genitricis memoriam agimus; intercessionis eius auxilio, a nostris iniquitatibus
resurgamus. Per eundem Christum Dominum nostrum.
Amen.

Regina Cæli
(Queen of Heaven)

The Regina Cæli is one of the four seasonal antiphons of the Blessed Virgin Mary, traditionally sung during the Easter Season, Holy Saturday to Pentecost, at the end of the final prayers of the day.

O Queen of heaven, rejoice! Alleluia.
For he whom you merited to bear, alleluia,
Has risen, as he said, alleluia.
Pray for us to God, alleluia.

℣. Rejoice and be glad, O Virgin Mary, alleluia.
℟. For the Lord has risen indeed, alleluia.

Let us pray.
God, who through the resurrection of thy Son, our Lord Jesus Christ, didst vouchsafe to fill the world with joy, grant we beseech thee, that through his virgin mother, Mary, we may lay hold on the joys of everlasting life. Through the same Christ our Lord.
Amen.

(In Latin)
Regina cæli, lætare! Alleluia.
Quia quem meruisti portare, alleluia.
Resurrexit, sicut dixit, alleluia.
Ora pro nobis Deum, alleluia.

℣. *Gaude et lætare, Virgo Maria, alleluia.*
℟. *Quia surrexit Dominus vere, alleluia.*

Oremus.
*Deus, qui per resurrectionem Filii tui, Domini nostri Iesu Christi, mundum
lætificare dignatus es: præsta, quæsumus; ut per eius Genetricem Virginem
Mariam, perpetuæ capiamus gaudia vitæ. Per eundem Christum Dominum
nostrum.*
Amen.

Salve, Regina
(Hail, Holy Queen)

The Salve, Regina *is one of the four seasonal antiphons of the Blessed Virgin Mary, traditionally sung from the end of the Easter season until Advent, at the end of the final prayers of the day.*

Hail, holy Queen, Mother of mercy,
our life, our sweetness, and our hope.

To thee do we cry, poor banished children of Eve;
to thee do we send up our sighs,
mourning and weeping in this valley of tears.

Turn, then, most gracious advocate,
thine eyes of mercy toward us;
and after this, our exile, show unto us
the blessed fruit of thy womb, Jesus;
O clement, O loving, O sweet Virgin Mary.

℣. Pray for us, O holy Mother of God.
℟. That we may be made worthy of the promises of Christ.

Let us pray.
Almighty, everlasting God, who by the cooperation of the
Holy Spirit didst prepare the body and soul of the glorious
Virgin Mother, Mary, to become the fit habitation of thy Son,
grant that we who now rejoice in her commemoration may,
by her gracious intercession, be delivered from all the evils
that threaten us and from everlasting death. Through the same
Christ our Lord.
Amen.

(In Latin)
Salve, Regina, mater misericordiæ;
vita, dulcedo et spes nostra, salve.

Ad te clamamus exsules filii Hevæ.
Ad te suspiramus gementes et flentes
in hac lacrimarum valle.

Eia ergo, advocata nostra,
illos tuos misericordes oculos ad nos converte.
Et Iesum, benedictum fructum ventris tui,
nobis post hoc exsilium ostende.
O clemens, o pia, o dulcis Virgo Maria.

℣.*Ora pro nobis, sancta Dei Genitrix.*
℟. *Ut digni efficamur promissionibus Christi.*

Oremus.
Omnipotens sempiterne Deus, qui gloriosæ Virginis Matris Mariæ corpus
et animam, ut dignum Filii tui habitaculum effici mereretur, Spiritu Sancto
cooperante, præparasti, da, ut cuius commemoratione lætamur; eius pia
intercessione, ab instantibus malis et a morte perpetua liberemur. Per eundem
Christum Dominum nostrum. Amen.

The Rosary

The Rosary is a prayer practice consisting of a sequence of repetitive prayers accompanying deeper meditation. The focus of the deeper reflection is the life and death of Christ. Praying the Rosary is considered a Marian practice because it is seen as focusing on Christ through Mary.

The term rosary applies to both the prayer practice and the beads commonly associated with it. While some rosary chains and rings have a single set of ten beads or bumps, the most common rosary, sometimes called the Dominican Rosary, has five sets of ten beads, plus larger beads between them, and a set of three small beads surrounded by two large beads ending in a crucifix for prayers at the beginning.

The usual prayer sequence is as follows:

- Hold the crucifix, make the sign of the cross, and say the Apostles' Creed.

- Move to the first large bead and say an Our Father. For each of the three small beads, say a Hail Mary. On the final large bead, say the Glory Be.

- Now move on to the main part of the rosary and for each decade:

    Hold the large bead, set the intention to meditate on a particular mystery, and say the Our Father.
    For each of the ten small beads, say a Hail Mary while continuing to meditate on the mystery.
    Finish by saying the Glory Be.
    (Some add here a prayer from Our Lady of Fátima:
        "O my Jesus, forgive us our sins, save us from the fires of hell, and lead all souls to Heaven, especially those who have most need of thy mercy.")

- Finish by saying the Salve, Regina (Hail, Holy Queen). (See previous section.)

From the sixteenth century until 2002, the format of the rosary prayer practice was unchanged in the Catholic Church, consisting of three sets of five mysteries: the Joyful Mysteries, the Sorrowful Mysteries, and the Glorious Mysteries, meditating on Jesus's birth, death, and resurrection, respectively. In 2002, Pope St. John Paul II added a fourth set, called the Luminous Mysteries and adapted from a version developed by St. George Preca, which brings into the rosary a set of meditations on the life of Jesus. A typical pattern is to meditate on the Joyful Mysteries on Monday and Saturday, the Sorrowful Mysteries on Tuesday and Friday, the Glorious Mysteries on Wednesday and Sunday, and the Luminous Mysteries on Thursday.

MYSTERIES OF THE ROSARY

Joyful Mysteries

The Annunciation

The Visitation

The Nativity

The Presentation in the Temple

The Finding of the Child Jesus after Three Days in the Temple

Luminous Mysteries

The Baptism at the Jordan

The Miracle at Cana

The Proclamation of the Kingdom and the Call to Conversion

The Transfiguration

The Institution of the Eucharist

Sorrowful Mysteries

The Agony in the Garden

The Scourging at the Pillar

The Crowning with Thorns

The Carrying of the Cross

The Crucifixion and Death

Glorious Mysteries

The Resurrection

The Ascension

The Descent of the Holy Spirit at Pentecost

The Assumption of Mary

The Crowning of the Blessed Virgin as Queen of Heaven and Earth

Prayers
by Saints

A Prayer for Every Family on Earth

Lord God, from you every family in heaven and on earth takes its name. Father, you are Love and Life.

Through your Son, Jesus Christ, born of woman, and through the Holy Spirit, fountain of divine charity, grant that every family on earth may become for each successive generation a true shrine of life and love.

Grant that your grace may guide the thoughts and actions of husbands and wives for the good of their families and of all the families in the world.

Grant that the young may find in the family solid support for their human dignity and for their growth in truth and love.

Grant that love, strengthened by the grace of the sacrament of marriage, may prove mightier than all the weakness and trials through which our families sometimes pass.

Through the intercession of the holy family of Nazareth, grant that the Church may fruitfully carry out her worldwide mission in the family and through the family.

We ask this of you, who are Life, Truth, and Love, with the Son and the Holy Spirit. Amen.

ST. TERESA OF CALCUTTA
Prayer for Our Family

Heavenly Father,
you have given us the model of life
in the holy family of Nazareth.
Help us, O Loving Father,
to make our family another Nazareth
where love, peace, and joy reign.
May it be deeply contemplative,
intensely Eucharistic,
revived with joy.

Help us to stay together in joy and sorrow in family prayer.
Teach us to see Jesus in the members of our families,
especially in their distressing disguise.

May the Eucharistic heart of Jesus
make our hearts humble like his
and help us to carry out our family duties in a holy way.

May we love one another as God loves each one of us,
more and more each day,
and forgive each other's faults
as you forgive our sins.

Help us, O Loving Father,
to take whatever you give
and give whatever you take
with a big smile.

Immaculate Heart of Mary,
cause of our joy, pray for us.
St. Joseph, pray for us.
Holy Guardian Angels,
be always with us,
guide and protect us.
Amen.

St. Patrick's Breastplate

A lorica is a Celtic Christian prayer you say to ask for God's protection from some enemy—including the Enemy. (The word lorica is Latin for upper body armor.) The best known lorica is commonly called St. Patrick's Breastplate. It dates back at least to the eighth century, and tradition assigns its authorship to St. Patrick in the fifth century, giving the prayer its common name. These exact lines or ones inspired by them have been used in numerous worship songs across many traditions. It is common to pray just the first five lines.

I arise today
 Through a mighty strength, the invocation of the Trinity,
 Through the belief in the threeness,
 Through confession of the oneness
 Of the Creator of Creation.

I arise today
 Through the strength of Christ's birth with his baptism,
 Through the strength of his crucifixion with his burial,
 Through the strength of his resurrection with his ascension,
 Through the strength of his descent for the judgment of Doom.

I arise today
 Through the strength of the love of Cherubim,
 In obedience of angels,
 In the service of archangels,
 In hope of resurrection to meet with reward,
 In prayers of patriarchs,
 In predictions of prophets,
 In preaching of apostles,
 In faith of confessors,
 In innocence of holy virgins,
 In deeds of righteous men.

I arise today
  Through the strength of heaven:
  Light of sun,
  Radiance of moon,
  Splendor of fire,
  Speed of lightning,
  Swiftness of wind,

  Depth of sea,
  Stability of earth,
  Firmness of rock.

I arise today
  Through God's strength to pilot me:
  God's might to uphold me,
  God's wisdom to guide me,
  God's eye to look before me,
  God's ear to hear me,
  God's word to speak for me,
  God's hand to guard me,
  God's way to lie before me,
  God's shield to protect me,
  God's host to save me
  From snares of devils,
  From temptations of vices,
  From everyone who shall wish me ill,
  Afar and anear,
  Alone and in multitude.

I summon today all these powers between me and those evils,
  Against every cruel and merciless power that may oppose
  my body and soul,
  Against incantations of false prophets,
  Against black laws of pagandom,

Against false laws of heretics,
Against craft of idolatry,
Against spells of witches and smiths and wizards,
Against every knowledge that corrupts man's body and soul.

Christ to shield me today
Against poison, against burning,
Against drowning, against wounding,
So that there may come to me abundance of reward.

Christ with me,
Christ before me,
Christ behind me,
Christ in me,
Christ beneath me,
Christ above me,
Christ on my right,
Christ on my left,
Christ when I lie down,
Christ when I sit down,
Christ when I arise,
Christ in the heart of every man who thinks of me,
Christ in the mouth of everyone who speaks of me,
Christ in every eye that sees me,
Christ in every ear that hears me.

I arise today
Through a mighty strength, the invocation of the Trinity,
Through belief in the threeness,
Through confession of the oneness
Of the Creator of Creation.

ST. IGNATIUS OF LOYOLA
Prayer for Generosity

Lord, teach me to be generous.
Teach me to serve you as you deserve;
to give and not to count the cost,
to fight and not to heed the wounds,
to toil and not to seek for rest,
to labor and not to ask for reward,
save that of knowing that I do your will.

Prayers
Through
Saints

Saints Michael, Gabriel, and Raphael, the Archangels

Heavenly King, you have given us archangels
to assist us during our pilgrimage on earth.

St. Michael is our protector;
I ask him to come to my aid [and the aid of _____],
fight for all my loved ones,
and protect us from danger.

St. Gabriel is a messenger of the Good News;
I ask him to help me [and _____]
to clearly hear your voice
and to teach me the truth.

St. Raphael is the healing angel;
I ask him to take my need for healing
and that of everyone I know [especially _____].
Lift it up to your throne of grace
and deliver back to us the gift of recovery.

Help us, O Lord,
to realize more fully the reality of the archangels
and their desire to serve us.
Holy angels, pray for us.
Amen.

ST. MAXIMILIAN KOLBE
for Family Struggling with Addiction

St. Maximilian Kolbe was a Polish Conventual Franciscan who, in Auschwitz, volunteered to take the place of a prisoner with a family and was starved, then executed by lethal injection. Pope St. John Paul II canonized him and declared him a martyr in 1982.

St. Maximilian Kolbe, your life of love and labor for souls was sacrificed amid the horrors of a concentration camp and hastened to its end by an injection of a deadly drug.

Look with compassion upon _____ who is now entrapped in addiction and whom we now recommend to your powerful intercession.

Having offered your own life to preserve that of a family man, we turn to you with trust, confident that you will understand and help.

Obtain for us the grace never to withhold our love and understanding, nor to fail in persevering prayer that the enslaving bonds of addiction may be broken and that full health and freedom may be restored to [him/her] whom we love.

We will never cease to be grateful to God who has helped us and heard your prayer for us. Amen.

ST. JUDE

Most holy Apostle, St. Jude, faithful servant and friend of Jesus, the Church honors and invokes you universally as the patron of hope.

Please intercede on my behalf. Make use of that particular privilege given to you to bring hope, comfort, and help where they are needed most.

Come to my assistance in this great need that I may receive the consolation and help of heaven as I work with my challenges, particularly (here make your request). I praise God with you and all the saints forever.

I promise, blessed St. Jude, to be ever mindful of this great favor, to always honor you as my special and powerful patron, and to gratefully encourage devotion to you.

Amen.

Special Prayers

Infant Jesus of Prague
Novena to the Infant Jesus of Prague

(Say daily for nine consecutive days or hourly for nine consecutive hours.)
Devotion to the Infant Jesus of Prague is especially common on the Feast of the
Holy Name of Jesus and during the Christmas season generally.

O Jesus, who said, "Ask and you shall receive, seek and you
shall find, knock and it shall be opened to you," through the
intercession of Mary, your most holy Mother, I knock, I seek,
I ask that my prayer be answered. [Make your request.]

O Jesus, who said, "All that you ask of the Father in my Name
he will grant you," through the intercession of Mary, your
most holy Mother, I humbly and urgently ask your Father in
your Name that my prayer be granted. [Make your request.]

O Jesus, who said, "Heaven and earth will pass away, but my
word shall not pass," through the intercession of Mary, your
most holy Mother, I feel confident that my prayer will be
granted. [Make your request.]

Divine Infant Jesus, I know you love me and would never leave
me. I thank you for your close Presence in my life.

Miraculous Infant, I believe in your promise of peace, blessings,
and freedom from want. I place every need and care in your
hands.

Lord Jesus, may I always trust in your generous mercy and love.
I want to honor and praise you, now and forever.

Amen.

Holy Family
Prayer to the Holy Family

Jesus, Mary, and Joseph,
in you we contemplate
the splendor of true love;
to you we turn with trust.

Holy family of Nazareth,
grant that our families too
may be places of communion and prayer,
authentic schools of the Gospel
and small domestic churches.

Holy family of Nazareth,
may families never again experience
violence, rejection, and division;
may all who have been hurt or scandalized
find ready comfort and healing.

Holy family of Nazareth,
make us once more mindful
of the sacredness and inviolability of the family,
and its beauty in God's plan.

Jesus, Mary, and Joseph,
graciously hear our prayer.

Amen.

Novena to the Holy Family

To be prayed for nine days from December 20 through the Feast of the Holy Family on December 28, or during February, the month of the holy family.

Jesus, Mary, and Joseph, bless me and grant me the grace of loving Holy Church as I should, above every earthly thing, and of ever showing my love by deeds.
Our Father, Hail Mary, Glory Be

Jesus, Mary, and Joseph, bless me and grant me the grace of openly professing as I should, with courage and without human respect, the faith that I received as your gift in holy Baptism.
Our Father, Hail Mary, Glory Be

Jesus, Mary, and Joseph, bless me and grant me the grace of sharing as I should in the defense and propagation of the Faith when duty calls, whether by word or by the sacrifice of my possessions and my life.
Our Father, Hail Mary, Glory Be

Jesus, Mary, and Joseph, bless me and grant me the grace of loving my family and others in mutual charity as I should, and establish us in perfect harmony of thought, will, and action, under the rule and guidance of the shepherds of the Church.
Our Father, Hail Mary, Glory Be

Jesus, Mary, and Joseph, bless me and grant me the grace of conforming my life fully as I should to the commandments of God's law and those of his Holy Church, so as to live always in that charity which they set forth.
Our Father, Hail Mary, Glory Be

Jesus, Mary, and Joseph, I ask in particular this special favor:

_____.

Amen.

Prayer for One's Family

Lord Jesus Christ, being subject to Mary and Joseph, you sanctified family life by your beautiful virtues. Grant that we, with the help of Mary and Joseph, may be taught by the example of your holy family, and may after death enjoy its everlasting companionship.

Lord Jesus, help us ever to follow the example of your holy family, that in the hour of our death your glorious Virgin Mother together with Saint Joseph may come to meet us, and we may be worthy to be received by you into the everlasting joys of heaven. You live and reign forever. Amen.

Sacred Heart of Jesus

Devotion to the Sacred Heart of Jesus is popular throughout the year in the Roman Catholic Church. The Solemnity of the Most Sacred Heart of Jesus is celebrated on the Friday nineteen days after Pentecost.

A Sacred Heart of Jesus Enthronement Ceremony can be performed in your home, consecrating your household to Jesus as its king. This is done with a priest, and gathered friends and family. An image of the Sacred Heart of Jesus is located in a place of honor in the home. The priest blesses the image and enthrones it in the home.

Once this initial ritual has been performed, the family can then reaffirm the consecration on the Solemnity of the Most Sacred Heart of Jesus and on the Feast of Christ the King, and with important family events—births, baptisms, anniversaries, first communions, joyous events, sorrows, and major transitions, such as when a child marries or leaves for college or service.

Prayer to the Sacred Heart of Jesus

O most holy heart of Jesus, fountain of every blessing, I adore you, I love you, and with lively sorrow for my sins I offer you this poor heart of mine. Make me humble, patient, pure, and wholly obedient to your will. Grant, Good Jesus, that I may live in you and for you. Protect me in the midst of danger. Comfort me in my afflictions. Give me health of body, assistance in my temporal needs, your blessing on all that I do, and the grace of a holy death. Amen.

Family Prayer of Thanksgiving to the Sacred Heart of Jesus

Glory be to you, O Sacred Heart of Jesus, for the infinite mercy you have bestowed upon the privileged members of this family. You have chosen it from thousands of others, as a recipient of your love and a sanctuary of reparation wherein your most loving Heart shall find consolation for the ingratitude of men. How great, O Lord Jesus, is the confusion of this portion of your faithful flock as we accept the unmerited honor of seeing you preside over our family!

Silently we adore you, overjoyed to see you sharing under the same roof the toils, cares, and joys of your children! It is true, we are not worthy that you should enter our humble abode, but you have already reassured us, when you did reveal your Sacred Heart to us, teaching us to find in the wound of your Sacred Side the source of grace and life everlasting. In this loving and trusting spirit, we give ourselves to you, you who are unchanging Life. Remain with us, Most Sacred Heart, for we feel an irresistible desire to love you and make you loved.

May our home be for you a haven as sweet as that of Bethany, where you can find rest in the midst of loving friends who, like Mary, have chosen the better part in the loving intimacy of your Heart! May this home be for you, O beloved Savior, a humble but hospitable refuge during the exile imposed on you by your enemies.

Come, then, Lord Jesus, come, for here as at Nazareth, we have a tender love for the Virgin Mary, your sweet Mother whom you have given us to be our Mother. Come, to fill with your sweet presence the vacancies which misfortune and death have wrought in our midst.

O most faithful Friend, had you been here in the midst of sorrow, our tears would have been less bitter; the comforting balm of peace would then have soothed these hidden wounds, which are known to you alone. Come, for even now perhaps, there is drawing near for us the twilight of tribulation, and the decline of the passing days of our youth and our illusions. Stay with us, for already it is late, and a perverted world seeks to envelop us in the darkness of its denials while we wish to adhere to you who alone are the Way, the Truth, and the Life. Repeat for us those words you said: "This day I must abide in this home."

Yes, dear Lord, take up your abode with us, so that we may live in your love and in your presence, we who proclaim you as our King and wish no other! May your triumphant Heart, O Jesus, be forever loved, blessed, and glorified in this home! Your kingdom come! Amen!

The Golden Arrow Prayer

In her 1843 autobiography, Carmelite nun Sr. Marie of St. Peter wrote of visions in which Jesus told her that sacrilege and blasphemy were like "poisoned arrows." This prayer is offered as an act of reparation.

May the most holy, most sacred, most adorable,
most incomprehensible and ineffable Name of God
be forever praised, blessed, loved, adored,
and glorified in Heaven, on earth,
and under the earth,
by all the creatures of God,
and by the Sacred Heart of Our Lord Jesus Christ,
in the Most Holy Sacrament of the Altar.
Amen.

Divine Mercy

In her diary, St. Faustina Kowalska of the Blessed Sacrament, OLM, recorded her experiences of apparitions of Jesus and the theme of devotion to the divine mercy of Jesus—asking for and trusting in Christ's mercy for us, and revealing God's love to others through showing mercy to them. Pope St. John Paul II, also from Poland, canonized Sister Faustina, and added devotion to Divine Mercy to the church's calendar, on the first Sunday after Easter.

Chaplet of the Divine Mercy
A chaplet is a prayer form using beads. You can use your usual rosary.

- Hold the crucifix and make the sign of the cross.
- Move to the first bead and say "You expired, Jesus, but the source of life gushed forth for souls, and the ocean of mercy opened up for the whole world. O Fount of Life, unfathomable Divine Mercy, envelop the whole world and empty yourself out upon us."
- Then say three times: "O Blood and Water, which gushed forth from the Heart of Jesus as a fountain of Mercy for us, I trust in you!"
- Move to the first small bead and say an Our Father. On the second, a Hail Mary. On the third, the Apostles' Creed.
- Now move on to the main part of the rosary and for each decade:
  Hold the large bead and say, "Eternal Father, I offer you the Body and Blood, Soul and Divinity of your dearly beloved Son, Our Lord, Jesus Christ, in atonement for our sins and those of the whole world."
  For each of the ten small beads say, "For the sake of his sorrowful Passion, have mercy on us and on the whole world." You can add other petitions for mercy here.

- To finish, holding the medallion, say three times, "Holy God, Holy Mighty One, Holy Immortal One, have mercy on us and on the whole world."

  Then say, "Eternal God, in whom mercy is endless and the treasury of compassion inexhaustible, look kindly upon us and increase your mercy in us, that in difficult moments we might not despair or become despondent, but with great confidence submit ourselves to your holy will, which is Love and Mercy itself."

- Offer any further intentions and finish by making the sign of the cross.

Novena of the Divine Mercy

You can pray the chaplet of the Divine Mercy as a novena, for nine days beginning on Good Friday, leading up to Divine Mercy Sunday.

Each day, say the Chaplet of the Divine Mercy, with your intention on a different group of people as follows:

1 All mankind, all sinners.

2 The souls of priests and the religious.

3 All devout and faithful people.

4 Those who do not believe in Jesus and those who do not yet know him.

5 The souls of separated brethren.

6 The souls of the meek and humble and of children.

7 The souls of people who especially glorify Jesus's mercy.

8 The souls in purgatory.

9 Souls who have become lukewarm.

Stations
of the Cross

In the very popular devotion of the Stations of the Cross, participants "walk" with Jesus through the key scenes of his suffering and death, from the point where he is condemned to die to the laying of his body in the tomb. It loosely matches the physical route of the Via Dolorosa in Jerusalem, and is sometimes called the Way of the Cross.

Cathedrals, and often churches and cloisters, have a series of paintings or sculptures the devout may walk through in doing this devotion. In this way, they are in a sense taking a virtual pilgrimage to the sites in Jerusalem. Many faithful pray the Stations of the Cross on Good Friday—the day on which the events took place—and some do so every Friday, or every Wednesday and Friday, during Lent, and at other times. The stations can be done alone, or in a group led by a celebrant.

Since the seventeenth century, the fourteen stations of the cross have been well set, though the prayers associated with each vary. They are:

1 Pilate condemns Jesus to die
2 Jesus accepts his cross
3 Jesus falls for the first time
4 Jesus meets his mother, Mary
5 Simon helps carry the cross
6 Veronica wipes the face of Jesus
7 Jesus falls for the second time
8 Jesus meets the three women of Jerusalem
9 Jesus falls for the third time
10 Jesus is stripped of his clothes
11 Jesus is nailed to the cross
12 Jesus dies on the cross
13 Jesus is taken down from the cross
14 Jesus is placed in the tomb

Prayer at Each Station of the Cross

We adore you, O Christ,
and we praise you,
because by your holy Cross you
have redeemed the world.

Stabat Mater

The Stabat Mater is a beautiful thirteenth-century hymn attributed to Franciscan friar Jacopone da Todi and put to music many times, most famously by Giovanni Battista Pergolesi in 1736. It describes Christ's Passion from the perspective of his mother, Mary, and is sung at Vespers on Good Friday, and sometimes with the Stations of the Cross.

The following is an English translation of the Latin hymn by Edward Caswall.

At the Cross her station keeping,
stood the mournful Mother weeping,
close to her Son to the last.

Through her heart, his sorrow sharing,
all his bitter anguish bearing,
now at length the sword has pass'd.

Oh, how sad and sore distress'd
was that Mother, highly blest,
of the sole-begotten One!

Christ above in torment hangs;
she beneath beholds the pangs
of her dying glorious Son.

Is there one who would not weep,
whelm'd in miseries so deep,
Christ's dear Mother to behold?

Can the human heart refrain
from partaking in her pain,
in that Mother's pain untold?

Bruised, derided, cursed, defiled,
She beheld her tender Child,
All with bloody scourges rent;

For the sins of his own nation,
Saw him hang in desolation,
Till his Spirit forth he sent.

O thou Mother! fount of love!
Touch my spirit from above,
make my heart with thine accord:

Make me feel as thou hast felt;
make my soul to glow and melt
with the love of Christ my Lord.

Holy Mother! pierce me through;
in my heart each wound renew
of my Savior crucified:

Let me share with thee his pain,
who for all my sins was slain,
who for me in torments died.

Let me mingle tears with thee,
mourning him who mourn'd for me,
all the days that I may live:

By the Cross with thee to stay,
there with thee to weep and pray,
is all I ask of thee to give.

Virgin of all virgins blest!
Listen to my fond request:
let me share thy grief divine;

Let me, to my latest breath,
in my body bear the death
of that dying Son of thine.

Wounded with his every wound,
steep my soul till it hath swoon'd,
in his very Blood away;

Be to me, O Virgin, nigh,
lest in flames I burn and die,
in his awful Judgment Day.

Christ, when thou shalt call me hence,
be thy Mother my defense,
be thy Cross my victory;

While my body here decays,
may my soul thy goodness praise,
Safe in Paradise with thee.

Stations of the Cross

Antiphon and Opening Prayer

We beseech thee, O Lord! to assist and direct our actions by
thy powerful grace, and all our prayers and works may always
begin and end with thee. Through Christ our Lord. Amen.

O Jesus, treasure of my soul, infinitely good, infinitely merciful,
behold me prostrate at thy sacred feet! Sinner as I am, I fly
to the arms of thy mercy, and implore that grace which
melts and converts—the grace of true compunction. I have
offended thee, adorable Jesus! I repent; let the favor of my
love equal the baseness of my ingratitude. This Way of the
Cross, grant me to offer devoutly in memory of that painful
journey thou hast travelled for our redemption, to the Cross
of Calvary, with the holy design to reform my morals, amend
my life, and gain these indulgences granted by thy vicars on
earth. I apply one for my miserable soul, the rest in suffrage
for the souls in purgatory, particularly *[here mention the souls for
whom you intend to apply them]*. I begin this devotion under thy
sacred protection, and in imitation of thy dolorous Mother.
Let then this holy exercise obtain for me mercy in this life,
and glory in the next. Amen. Jesus!

STATION 1
Christ Is Sentenced to Death by Pilate

℣. We adore thee, O Lord Jesus Christ, and bless thee.
℟. Because by thy holy Cross thou hast redeemed the world.

The Mystery

Our gracious Redeemer, after suffering blows and blasphemies before Annas and Caiphas, after the cruel scourging, insulting contempts, and bloody crown of piercing thorns, is unjustly condemned to death. This iniquitous sentence your Jesus accepted with admirable humility. Innocence embraces condemnation to free the guilty.

Reflect that your sins were the false witnesses that condemned him; your stubborn impenitence the tyrant that extorted from Pilate the bloody sentence.

Propose now seriously an amendment of life, and while you reflect on the horrid injustice of Pilate, who condemns innocence, lest he should not appear a friend of Caesar, arraign yourself for your many sins of human respect; think how often you have offended God for fear of displeasing the eye of the world, and turning your loving Jesus, addressed him rather with tears of the heart than with expressions of the tongue in the following:

Prayer

O mangled victim of my sins! O suffering Jesus! I have deserved those bloody scourges, that cruel sentence of death; and yet thou didst die for me, that I should live for thee. I am convinced that if I desire to please men, I cannot by thy servant. Let me then displease the world and its vain admirers. I resign myself into thy hands. Let love take possession of my heart; let my eyes behold with contempt everything that can alienate my affections from thee; let my ears be ever attentive to thy word;

let me through this painful journey accompany thee, sighing and demanding mercy. Mercy! Jesus! Amen.

Our Father, Hail Mary, and Glory Be

Jesus Christ crucified, have mercy on us!

You pious Christians who do now draw near,
With relenting hearts now lend a tear,
Your Lord behold with great humility,
Sentenced to die on Mount Calvary.

STATION 2
Christ Takes the Cross on His Shoulder

℣. We adore thee, O Lord Jesus Christ, and bless thee.
℟. Because by thy holy Cross thou hast redeemed the world.

The Mystery

This second Station represents the place where your most
amiable Redeemer is clad in his usual attire, after his inhuman
executioners had stripped him of the purple garment of
derision with which he was clothed, when as a visionary king
they crowned him with plaited thorns. The heavy burden of
the Cross is violently placed on his mangled shoulders.

Behold your gracious Savior, though torn with wounds, covered
with blood, a man of griefs, abandoned by all—with what
silent patience he bears the taunts and injuries with which he
was insulted. He stretches out his bleeding arms, and tenderly
embraces the Cross.

Reflect with confusion on that sensitive pride which is fired
with impatience at the very shadow of contempt—on your
discontented murmurs in your lightest afflictions—and your
obstinate resistance to the will of Heaven in the crosses of
life, which are calculated to conduct you, not to a Calvary of
Crucifixion, but to joys of eternal glory; and from your heart
unite in the following:

Prayer

Meek and humble Jesus, my iniquity and perverseness loaded
thy shoulders with the heavy burden of the Cross. Yet I, a
vile worm of the earth—O shameful ingratitude!—fly even
the appearance of mortification, and everything which would
check the violence of my passions; and if I suffered, it was with
a murmuring reluctance. I now, O Saviour of the world, detest
my past life, and by thy grace am determined no more to offend

thee mortally. Let me only glory in the Cross of my Lord, by whom the world is crucified to me, and I to the world. Lay then on my stubborn neck the cross of true penance; let me, for the love of thee, bear the adversities of this life, and cleave inseparably to thee in the bonds of perpetual charity. Amen, Jesus.

Our Father, Hail Mary, and Glory Be

Jesus Christ crucified, have mercy on us!

No pity for the Lamb was to be found;
As a mock King my loving Lord they crown'd,
To bear the heavy cross he does not tire,
To save my soul from everlasting fire.

STATION 3
Jesus Falls the First Time under the Cross

℣. We adore thee, O Lord Jesus Christ, and bless thee.
℞. Because by thy holy Cross thou hast redeemed the world.

The Mystery

This third Station represents how our Lord Jesus Christ,
overwhelmed by the weight of the Cross, fainting through
loss of blood, falls to the ground the first time.

Contemplate the unwearied patience of the meek Lamb, amidst
the insulting blows and curses of his brutal executioners;
while you, impatient in adversity and infirmity, presume to
complain, nay, to insult the Majesty of Heaven, by your
curses and blasphemies. Purpose here firmly to struggle
against the impatient sallies of temper; and beholding your
amiable Jesus prostrate under the Cross, excite in yourself
your Savior, who for love of you, was burdened, and thus you
afflicted Jesus.

Prayer

Alas, my Jesus! the merciless violence of thy inhuman
executioners, the excessive weight of the Cross, or rather
the more oppressive load of my sins, crush thee to the earth.
Panting for breath, exhausted as thou art, thou dost not refuse
new tortures for me. Will I then refuse the light burden of thy
commandments; will I refuse to do violence to my perverse
passions and sinful attachments; will I relapse into those very
crimes for which I have shed false and delusive tears? O Jesus!
stretch thy holy hand to my assistance, that I may never more
fall into mortal sin; that I may at the hour of my death secure
the important affair of my salvation. Amen, Jesus.

Our Father, Hail Mary, and Glory Be

Jesus Christ crucified, have mercy on us!

From loss of blood he fell unto the ground,
No comfort for my Lord was to be found,
He rose again beneath their cruel blows,
And on his bitter way unmurmuring goes.

STATION 4
Jesus, Carrying the Cross, Meets His Most Afflicted Mother

℣. We adore thee, O Lord Jesus Christ, and bless thee.
℟. Because by thy holy Cross thou hast redeemed the world.

The Mystery

This fourth Station represents to your contemplation the
meeting of the desolate Mother and her bleeding Jesus,
staggering under the weight of the Cross.

Consider what pangs rent her soul, when she beheld her
beloved Jesus covered with blood, dragged violently to the
place of execution, reviled and blasphemed by an ungrateful,
outrageous rabble. Meditate on her inward feelings, the looks
of silent agony exchanged between the Mother and the Son;
her anguish in not being permitted to approach, to embrace,
and to accompany him to death.

Filled with confusion at the thought that neither the Son's pains
nor the Mother's grief have softened the hardness of your heart,
contritely join in the following:

Prayer

O Mary! I am the cause of thy sufferings. O refuge of sinners! let
me participate in these heart-felt pangs, which rent thy tender soul,
when thou didst behold thy Son trembling with cold, covered with
wounds, fainting under the Cross, more dead than alive! Mournful
Mother! fountain of love! let me feel the force of thy grief that
I may weep with thee, and mingle my tears with thine, and thy
Son's blood. O suffering Jesus! by thy bitter passion, and the
heart-breaking compassion of thy afflicted Mother, grant me the
efficacious grace of perseverance! Mother of Jesus, intercede for
me! Jesus, behold me with an eye of pity, and in the hour of my
death receive me to the arms of thy mercy! Amen, Jesus.

Our Father, Hail Mary, and Glory Be

Jesus Christ crucified, have mercy on us!

Exhausted, spent, see Jesus onward go,
With feeble step, in anguish faint and slow,
At last his grief-worn Mother he can see
Exclaiming: my Son, my heart is rent for thee.

STATION 5
Christ Assisted by Simon the Cyrenean to Carry the Cross

℣. We adore thee, O Lord Jesus Christ, and bless thee.
℟. Because by thy holy Cross thou hast redeemed the world.

The Mystery

This fifth Station represents Christ fainting, destitute of
strength, unable to carry the Cross. His sacrilegious
executioners compel Simon the Cyrenean to carry it, not
through compassionate pity to Jesus, but lest he should expire
in their hand, before they could glut their vengeance by
nailing him to the Cross.

Consider here the repugnance of Simon to carry the Cross after
Christ; and that you with repugnance, and by compulsion,
carry the Cross that Providence has placed on your shoulders.
Will you spurn the love of your Jesus, who invites you to take
up your Cross and follow him? Will you yet with shameless
ingratitude refuse the Cross, sanctified by his suffering?

Offer up devoutly the following:

Prayer

O suffering Jesus! to what excess did thy impious executioners'
cruelty proceed, beholding thee faint under the Cross that
thou mightest expire on it in the most exquisite torture. But
why should I complain of the cruelty of the crowds or the
repugnance of Simon? Have I not again crucified thee by my
crimes? Have I not suffered with fretful impatience the light
afflictions with which thy mercy visited me? Inspire me not, my
Jesus, to detest and deplore my sinful impatience, my ungrateful
murmurs, and let me with all my heart cheerfully accompany
thee to Mount Calvary; let me live in thee, and die in thee.
Amen, Jesus.

Our Father, Hail Mary, and Glory Be

Jesus Christ crucified, have mercy on us!

The furious crowds when Jesus fainting fell,
Simon to bear his Cross, by force compel;
Afflictions bear like Job most patiently,
And follow the Lamb with great humility.

STATION 6
Veronica Presents a Handkerchief to Christ

℣. We adore thee, O Lord Jesus Christ, and bless thee.
℟. Because by thy holy Cross thou hast redeemed the world.

The Mystery

This sixth Station represents the place where the pious
Veronica, compassioning our agonizing Redeemer, beholding
his sacred face livid with blows and covered with blood and
sweat, presents a handkerchief, with which Jesus wipes his
face.

Consider the heroic piety of this devout woman, who is not
intimidated by the presence of the executioners, or the
clamor of the crowds; and the tender acknowledgment
of Jesus. Reflect here, that though you cannot personally
discharge the debt of humanity to your Savior, you can
discharge it to his suffering members, the poor. Though you
cannot wipe away the blood and sweat from the face of Jesus,
you can wipe away the tear of wretchedness from the eye of
misery.

Examine, then, what returns you have made from the singular
graces and favors your bountiful Jesus bestowed on you; and
conscious of your ingratitude, address your injured Savior in
the following:

Prayer

O Jesus, grant me tears to weep my ingratitude. How often
have I, infatuated wretch, turned my eyes from thee and thy
sufferings, to fix them on the world and its vanities! Let me
henceforth be Thine without division. Stamp thy image on my
soul, that it may never admit another love. Take possession of
my heart on earth, that my soul may take eternal possession of
thee in glory. Amen, Jesus.

Our Father, Hail Mary, and Glory Be

Jesus Christ crucified, have mercy on us!

Veronica pressed through to meet our Lord,
His streaming face a napkin to afford,
Lo, on its texture stamped by power divine
His sacred features breathe in every line.

STATION 7
Jesus Falls under the Cross the Second Time

℣. We adore thee, O Lord Jesus Christ, and bless thee.

℟. Because by thy holy Cross thou hast redeemed the world.

The Mystery

This seventh Station represents the gate of Jerusalem, called
the gate of Judgment, at the entrance of which our Savior,
through anguish and weakness, falls to the ground. He is
compelled by blows and blasphemies to rise.

Consider your Jesus prostrate on the earth, bruised by his fall,
and ignominiously treated by an ungrateful rabble. Reflect
that your self-love and pride of preference were the cause of
this humiliation. Implore, then, grace to detest sincerely your
haughty spirit and proud disposition. It was your reiterated
sins which again pressed him to the ground. Will you then sin
again, and add to the afflictions of your gracious Savior?

Prayer

O Most Holy Redeemer! treated with the utmost contempt,
deprived of fame and honor—led out to punishment—through
excess of torments, and the weakness of thy delicate and
mangled body, thou didst fall a second time to the earth. What
impious hand has prostrated thee? Alas, my Jesus! I am that
impious, that sacrilegious offender: my ambitious pride, my
haughty indignation, my contempt of others humbled by thee
to the earth. Banish forever from my mind the unhappy spirit of
pride. Teach my heart the doctrine of humility, so that detesting
pride, vain glory, and human respect, I may forever be united
with thee, my meek and humble Jesus. Amen.

Our Father, Hail Mary, and Glory Be

Jesus Christ crucified, have mercy on us!

Prone at the city gate he fell once more,
To save our erring souls he suffered sore;
On his great mercy let us always call,
Since our vain pride has caused his triple fall.

STATION 8
Christ Consoles the Women of Jerusalem, Who Wept over Him

℣. We adore thee, O Lord Jesus Christ, and bless thee.
℟. Because by thy holy Cross thou hast redeemed the world.

The Mystery

This eighth Station represents the place where several devout
women, meeting Jesus, and beholding him wounded and
bathed in his blood, shed tears of compassion over him.
Consider the excessive love of Jesus, who, though languishing
and half dead through the multitude of his torments, is
nevertheless attentive to console the women who wept over
him. They merited that tender consolation from the mouth
of Jesus, "Weep not over me, but over yourselves and your
children." Weep for your sins, the sources of my affliction.
Yes, O my soul! I will obey my suffering Lord, and pour out
tears of compassion. Nothing is more eloquent than the voice
of those tears which flow from the horror of those sins.
Address him the following:

Prayer

O Jesus, only begotten Son of the Father! who will give water
to my head, and a fountain of tears to my eyes, that I may day
and night weep and lament my sins? I humbly beseech thee
by these tears of blood thou didst shed for me, to soften my
flinty bosom, that tears may plentifully flow from my eyes,
and contrition rend my heart, this hardened heart, to cancel
my crimes and render me secure in the day of wrath and
examination, when thou wilt come to judge the living and the
dead, and demand a rigorous account of thy blood. Amen, Jesus.

Our Father, Hail Mary, and Glory Be

Jesus Christ crucified, have mercy on us!

With tears of love the women they did weep,
Compassioning our Redeemer sweet;
Weep for your sins who caused him here to be
O Lamb of God thy mercy show to me.

STATION 9
Jesus Falls under the Cross the Third Time

℣. We adore thee, O Lord Jesus Christ, and bless thee.
℟. Because by thy holy Cross thou hast redeemed the world.

The Mystery

This ninth Station represents the foot of Mount Calvary, where Jesus Christ, quite destitute of strength, falls a third time to the ground. The anguish of his wounds is renewed.

Consider here the many injuries and blasphemous derisions thrown out against Christ, to compel him to rise and hasten to the place of execution, that his inveterate enemies might enjoy the savage satisfaction of beholding him expire on the Cross. Consider that by your sins you daily hurry him to the place of execution. Approach him in thought to the foot of Mount Calvary, and cry out against the accursed weight of sin that prostrated Jesus, and had long since buried thee in the flames of hell, if his mercy and the merits of his passion had not preserved thee.

Prayer

O clement Jesus! I return thee infinite thanks for not permitting me, ungrateful sinner, as thou hast permitted thousands less criminal, to die in their sins. I, who have added torments to thy torments, by heaping sin on sin, kindle in my soul the fire of charity, fan it with thy continual grace into perseverance, until, delivered from the body of this death, I can enjoy the liberty of the children of God and thy co-heirs. Amen, Jesus!

Our Father, Hail Mary, and Glory Be

Jesus Christ crucified, have mercy on us!

On Calvary's height a third time see him fall,
Livid with bruises that our sight appal.
O gracious Lord, this sufferest thou for me,
To save my soul from endless misery.

STATION 10
Jesus Is Stripped of His Garments and Offered Vinegar and Gall

℣. We adore thee, O Lord Jesus Christ, and bless thee.
℟. Because by thy holy Cross thou hast redeemed the world.

The Mystery

This tenth Station represents how our Lord Jesus Christ ascended Mount Calvary, and was by his inhuman executioners stripped of his garments. The skin and congealed blood are torn off with them, and his wounds renewed.

Consider the confusion of the modest Lamb, exposed naked to the contempt and derision of an insulting rabble. They present him with vinegar and gall for a refreshment. Condemn here that delicacy of taste, that sensual indulgence, with which you flatter your sinful body. Pray here for the spirit of the Christian mortification. Think how happy you would die if, stripped of the world and its attachments, you could expire covered with the blood and agony of Jesus.

Prayer

Suffering Jesus! I behold thee stripped of thy garments, thy old wounds renewed, and new ones added to the old. I behold thee naked in the presence of thousands, exposed to the inclemency of the weather; cold, trembling from head to foot, insulted by the blasphemous derisions of the spectators. Strip, O mangled Lamb of God! my heart of the world and its deceitful affections. Divest my soul of its habits of sensual indulgence. Embitter the poisoned cup of pleasure, that I may dash it with contempt from my lips, and through Christian mortification arrive at thy never fading glory. Amen, Jesus!

Our Father, Hail Mary, and Glory Be

Jesus Christ crucified, have mercy on us!

O Queen of angels, how thy heart did bleed
To see thy Son stripped naked here indeed,
And to the vile and cruel throng exposed,
Who round him now in furious hatred closed.

STATION 11
Christ Is Nailed to the Cross

℣. We adore thee, O Lord Jesus Christ, and bless thee.
℟. Because by thy holy Cross thou hast redeemed the world.

The Mystery

This eleventh Station represents the place where Jesus Christ, in the presence of his afflicted mother, is stretched on the Cross, and nailed to it. How insufferable the torture—the nerves and sinews are rent by the nails.

Consider the exceeding desolation, the anguish of the tender Mother, eye-witness of this inhuman punishment of her beloved Jesus. Generously resolve then to crucify your criminal desires, and nail your sins to the wood of the Cross. Contemplate the suffering resignation of the Son of God to the will of his Father, while you are impatient in trifling afflictions, in trivial disappointments. Purpose henceforth to embrace your cross with ready resignation to the will of God.

Prayer

O patient Jesus! meek Lamb of God! who promised, "When I shall be exalted from earth I will draw all things to myself," attract my heart to thee, and nail it the Cross. I now renounce and detest my past impatience. Let me crucify my flesh with its concupiscence and vices. Here burn, here cut, but spare me for eternity. I throw myself into the arms of thy mercy. Thy will be done in all things. Grant me resignation, grant me thy love, I desire no more. Amen, Jesus!

Our Father, Hail Mary, and Glory Be

Jesus Christ crucified, have mercy on us!

You Christian hearts now join with Mary's grief;
Heaven and earth behold! deny relief;
Her heart was pierced with bitter grief to see
Her loving Jesus nailed unto a tree.

STATION 12
Christ Is Exalted on the Cross, and Dies

℣. We adore thee, O Lord Jesus Christ, and bless thee.
℞. Because by thy holy Cross thou hast redeemed the world.

The Mystery

This twelfth Station represents the place where Jesus Christ
was publicly exalted on the Cross between two robbers, who,
for their enormous crimes, were executed with the innocent
Lamb.

Consider here the confusion of your Savior, exposed naked
to the profane view of a blasphemous multitude. Imagine
yourself at the foot of the Cross. Behold that sacred body
streaming blood from every part. Contemplate the divine
countenance pale and languid, the heart throbbing in the
last pangs of agony, the soul on the point of separation;
yet charity triumphs over his agony; his last prayers
petition forgiveness of his enemies: "Father, forgive them,
for they know not what they do." His clemency is equally
extended to the penitent thief: "This day shalt thou be with
me in Paradise." He recommends in his last moments his
disconsolate Mother to his beloved St. John. He recommends
his soul to his heavenly Father, and bowing down his
submissive, obedient head, resigns his spirit. Turn your eyes
on the naked, bloody portrait of charity. Number his wounds.
Wash them with tears of sympathizing love. Behold the arms
extended to embrace you. Love of Jesus! thou diest to deliver
us from eternal captivity.

Prayer

O suffering Son of God! I now behold thee in last convulsive
pangs of death—thy veins opened, thy sinews torn, thy
hands and feet, O Fountain of Paradise! distilling blood. I

acknowledge, charitable Jesus, that my reiterated offenses
have been thy merciless executioners, the cause of thy bitter
sufferings and death. Yet, God of mercy, look on my sinful
soul, bathe it in thy precious blood! Let me die to vanity of the
world, and renounce its false pleasures. Thou didst pray, my
Jesus, for thy enemies. I forgive mine. I embrace them in the
bowels of thy charity. I bury my resentment in thy wounds.
Shelter me in the day of wrath in the sanctuary of thy side. Let
me live, let me die, in my crucified Jesus. Amen.

Our Father, Hail Mary, and Glory Be

Jesus Christ crucified, have mercy on us!

Behold the streams of blood from every part,
Behold the sharp lance that pierc'd his Sacred Heart;
On Calvary's Mount behold him naked hang,
To suffer for our sins pain's utmost pang.

STATION 13
Christ Is Taken Down from the Cross

℣. We adore thee, O Lord Jesus Christ, and bless thee.
℟. Because by thy holy Cross thou hast redeemed the world.

The Mystery

This thirteenth Station represents the place where Christ's most
  sacred body was taken down from the Cross by Joseph and
  Nicodemus, and laid in the bosom of his weeping Mother.
Consider the sighs and tears of the Virgin Mother, with what
  pangs she embraced the bloody remains of her beloved Jesus.
  Here unite your tears with those of the disconsolate Mother.
  Reflect that your Jesus would not descend from the Cross
  until he consummated the work of redemption; and that at his
  departure from, as well as at his entrance into the world, he
  would be placed in the bosom of his beloved Mother. Hence
  learn constancy in your pious resolutions! Cleave to the
  standard of the Cross. Consider with what purity that soul
  should be adorned which receives, in the blessed Sacrament
  of the Eucharist, Christ's most sacred body and blood.

Prayer

At length, O Blessed Virgin! Mother of sorrow! thou art
permitted to embrace thy beloved Son. But alas! the fruit of
thy immaculate womb is all over mangled, in one continued
wound. Yes, O Lord! the infernal fury of the crowds has at
length triumphed; yet we renew their barbarity, crucifying thee
by our sins, inflicting new wounds. Most afflicted mother of
my Redeemer, I conjure thee by the pains and torments thou
sufferest in the common cause of Salvation, to obtain for me, by
thy powerful intercession, pardon of my sins, and grace to weep
with a sympathizing feeling, thine and thy Son's afflictions.
As often as I appear at the Holy Sacrifice of the Mass, let

me embrace thee, my Jesus, in the bosom of my heart. May I worthily receive thee as the sacred pledge of my salvation. Amen, Jesus.

Our Father, Hail Mary, and Glory Be

Jesus Christ crucified, have mercy on us!

When from the Cross they took the blessed form,
His Mother cries, my Son, I am forlorn;
My child is dead, you virgins join with me,
Bewail in tears my love's sad destiny.

STATION 14
Christ Is Laid in the Holy Sepulchre

℣. We adore thee, O Lord Jesus Christ, and bless thee.
℞. Because by thy holy Cross thou hast redeemed the world.

The Mystery

This fourteenth Station represents Christ's Sepulchre, where his
blessed body was laid with piety and devotion.

Consider the emotions of the Virgin—her eyes streaming with
tears, her bosom heaving with sighs. What melancholy, what
wistful looks she cast on that monument where treasure of
her soul, her Jesus, her all, lay entombed. Here lament your
want of contrition for your sins, and humbly adore your
deceased Lord, who, poor even in death, is buried in another's
tomb. Blush at your dependence on the world, at the eager
solicitude with which you labor to grasp its perishable
advantages. Despise henceforth the world, lest you perish
with it.

Prayer

Charitable Jesus, for my salvation thou performedst the painful
journey of the Cross. Let me press the footsteps marked by
thee, gracious Redeemer—the paths which, through the thorns
of life, conduct to the heavenly Jerusalem. Would that thou
wert entombed in my heart, that being united to thee, I might
rise to a new life of grace, and persevere to the end. Grant me,
in my last moments, to receive thy precious Body, as the pledge
of immortal life. Let my last words be *Jesus and Mary*, my last
breath be united to thy last breath on the Cross; that with a
lively faith, a firm hope and ardent love, I may die with thee
and for thee; that I may reign with thee for ever and ever.
Amen, Jesus.

Our Father, Hail Mary, and Glory Be

Jesus Christ crucified, have mercy on us!

You pious Christians, raise your voices, raise,
And join with me to sing your Savior's praise,
Who shed his blood for us and died in pain,
To save our souls from hell's eternal flame.

Closing Prayer

Compassionate Jesus! behold with eyes of mercy this devotion I have endeavored to perform, in honor of thy bitter passion and death, in order to obtain remission of my sins, and the pains incurred by them. Accept of it for the salvation of the living and the eternal repose of the faithful departed, particularly for those whom I directed it. Do not, my Jesus, suffer the ineffable price of thy blood to be fruitless, nor my miserable soul ransomed by it, to perish. The voice of thy blood is louder for mercy than my crimes for vengeance. Have mercy then, O Lord! have mercy, and spare me for thy mercy's sake! Amen, Jesus.

The Peace Prayer

Lord, make me an instrument of your peace:
where there is hatred, let me sow love;
where there is injury, pardon;
where there is doubt, faith;
where there is despair, hope;
where there is darkness, light;
where there is sadness, joy.

O Divine Master, grant that I may not so much seek
to be consoled as to console,
to be understood as to understand,
to be loved as to love.
For it is in giving that we receive,
it is in pardoning that we are pardoned,
and it is in dying that we are born to eternal life.
Amen.

NOTES

33   *Fr. Edward Caswell*   Third Plenary Council of Baltimore, *A Manual of Prayers for the Use of the Catholic Laity*. (London: Burns & Oates, Ltd., 1888), 76–81.

68   *Prayer to the Holy Family*   Pope Francis, *Amoris Lætitia, Apostolic Exhortation on Love in the Family* (Vatican City: Libreria Editrice Vaticana, 2016), 255–256.

82   *English translation*   Edward Caswall, *Lyra Catholica* (London: E. Dunigan, 1849), 182–186.

84   *Stations of the cross*   *Illustrated Roman Catholic Douay Rheims Family Bible*, unabridged Haydock notes (New York: M. R. Gately, 1885).

112   *Amen, Jesus*   These Stations are the traditional, long-held ones of Christian devotion. In 2007, Pope Benedict XVI approved a new version of the fourteen Stations, all with references to the Gospel accounts.

About Paraclete Press

Who We Are

Paraclete Press is a publisher of books, recordings, and DVDs on Christian spirituality. Our publishing represents a full expression of Christian belief and practice—from Catholic to Evangelical, from Protestant to Orthodox.

We are the publishing arm of the Community of Jesus, an ecumenical monastic community in the Benedictine tradition. As such, we are uniquely positioned in the marketplace without connection to a large corporation and with informal relationships to many branches and denominations of faith.

What We Are Doing

PARACLETE PRESS BOOKS | Paraclete publishes books that show the richness and depth of what it means to be Christian. Although Benedictine spirituality is at the heart of all that we do, we publish books that reflect the Christian experience across many cultures, time periods, and houses of worship. We publish books that nourish the vibrant life of the church and its people.

We have several different series, including the bestselling Paraclete Essentials and Paraclete Giants series of classic texts in contemporary English; Voices from the Monastery—men and women monastics writing about living a spiritual life today; award-winning poetry; bestselling gift books for children on the occasions of baptism and first communion; and the Active Prayer Series that brings creativity and liveliness to any life of prayer.

MOUNT TABOR BOOKS | Paraclete's newest series, Mount Tabor Books, focuses on the arts and literature as well as liturgical worship and spirituality, and was created in conjunction with the Mount Tabor Ecumenical Centre for Art and Spirituality in Barga, Italy.

PARACLETE RECORDINGS | From Gregorian chant to contemporary American choral works, our recordings celebrate the best of sacred choral music composed through the centuries that create a space for heaven and earth to intersect. Paraclete Recordings is the record label representing the internationally acclaimed choir Gloriæ Dei Cantores, praised for their "rapt and fathomless spiritual intensity" by *American Record Guide*; the Gloriæ Dei Cantores Schola, specializing in the study and performance of Gregorian chant; and the other instrumental artists of the Arts Empowering Life Foundation.

Paraclete Press is also privileged to be the exclusive North American distributor of the recordings of the Monastic Choir of St. Peter's Abbey in Solesmes, France, long considered to be a leading authority on Gregorian chant.

PARACLETE VIDEO | Our DVDs offer spiritual help, healing, and biblical guidance for a broad range of life issues including grief and loss, marriage, forgiveness, facing death, bullying, addictions, Alzheimer's, and spiritual formation.

Learn more about us at our website:
www.paracletepress.com or phone us
toll-free at 1.800.451.5006

SCAN
TO
READ
MORE

You may also be interested in these books by Donna-Marie Cooper O'Boyle
— award-winning author, speaker, columnist,
EWTN television host, Catholic wife, mother of five, and grandmother.

A Catholic Woman's Book of Prayers

978-1-61261-921-7 $11.99 Trade paper

Donna-Marie is well aware of the difficulties women face today as they balance all their responsibilities and struggle to find time for prayer. This book will affirm women on their journey while celebrating the strength, dignity, and specific gifts of women in the context of their faith. Women from all walks of life will know that they are deeply loved by Christ, and that they share this journey with their sisters.

Feeding Your Family's Soul

978-1-61261-835-7 $15.99 Trade paper

This book is a vital tool to enable parents to transform a regular dinner time into a prayerful faith lesson for their elementary school to high school-aged children! Through 52 fun and creative faith lessons, this one-of-a-kind book will encourage parents and caregivers to seize the opportunity to teach the Catholic faith to children while gathered at the dinner table, reminding them of the value of coming together as a family to break bread and share hearts.

Feeding Your Family's Soul DVD

978-1-61261-971-2 $59.99 DVD

Feeling overwhelmed or unqualified to provide faith formation for your children? Join one of today's most devoted educators as she encourages parents with practical, meaningful ways to teach lessons of faith. With compassion and humor, Donna-Marie empowers parents to reclaim their role as the primary catechists of their children with seven inspiring lessons on love, prayer, forgiveness, the virtues, the Blessed Mother, and more!